POISON! BEWARE!

BY STEVE SKIDMORE
ILLUSTRATIONS BY THOMPSON YARDLEY

POISON! BEWARE!

THE MILLBROOK PRESS · BROOKFIELD, CONNECTICUT

Cataloging-in-Publication Data

Skidmore, Steve
Poison! Beware! be an ace poison spotter/
by Steve Skidmore; illustrations by Thompson Yardley.
Brookfield, Conn.: The Millbrook Press, 1991.
40 p.: col. ill.;   cm   (A lighter look book)
Includes bibliographical references (p. 39)
Includes index.
Summary: Discusses different kinds of
poisonous substances, animals and plants.
1. Poisons—Juvenile literature. 2. Toxicology—
Juvenile literature. I. Yardley, Thompson, ill.
II. Title. III. Series.
ISBN 1-878841-29-7

First published in the United States in 1991 by
The Millbrook Press
2 Old New Milford Road
Brookfield, Connecticut 06804
© Copyright Cassell plc 1990
First published in Great Britain in 1990 by
Cassell Publishers Limited

POISON! BEWARE!

WATCH OUT!

DEADLY POISONS ARE WAITING
AROUND EVERY CORNER!

They're in your home
and in the garden.
Shops are full of them!

Find out how to spot a deadly poison!
Find out how to save a poisoned person!

Find out how to beat deadly germs!
Find out how to beat the food scientists!

POISON POINTS

Each year in America over 6,300 people die through poisoning!

Boys are more likely to be accidentally poisoned than girls!

Years ago, kings and queens were afraid of being poisoned. So they used people called food tasters, who tasted the food to see if it was safe to eat.

WHAT IS POISON?

Another word for poisonous is TOXIC.
So if something is NONTOXIC, it's not poisonous.

Most crayons are nontoxic in case young children chew them!

Watch for the words TOXIC and NONTOXIC on things around your house or school! Poisonous products are required to carry warning labels. There are symbols that mean "poisonous," too.

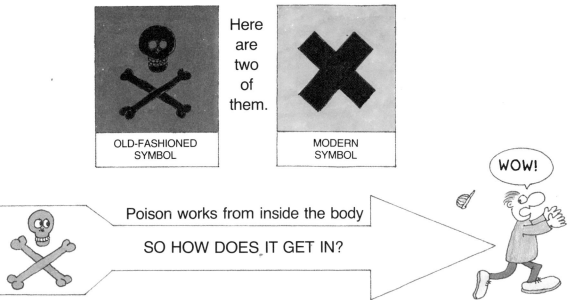

HOW POISONS ENTER YOUR BODY

BY BREATHING . . .

You can be poisoned by fumes from cars and factories.

THROUGH THE SKIN . . .

Poison can get into your skin just like water soaking into a sponge! Some chemicals that gardeners use act like this. Be careful when you handle soil and plants.

THROUGH A HOLE IN THE SKIN . . .

Poisons get into the body through holes in the skin, such as cuts or scrapes.

HOW POISONS ENTER YOUR BODY

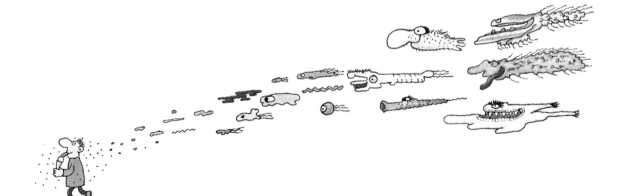

FROM GERMS . . .

Some germs that live in food give off deadly poisons.

Take a look at page 34 . . .

I think I'll have a glass of lemonade!

BLEACH

BY SWALLOWING . . .

This is the most common way that people are poisoned. It's easy to swallow poison by mistake, even in your own home.

Take a look . . .

SPOT THE POISONS!

Here's an ordinary house.
How many of the numbered items are poisonous?

HOW TO STOP ACCIDENTAL POISONINGS

There are two easy things to do:

1. Check that poisons are out of reach of young children. They might think they're good to eat or drink!

Make sure that all lids are on bottles and cans, and put them in a high cupboard . . .

but not too high!

2. Never put poison into a bottle with the wrong label on it. Lots of people have been poisoned by weed killer that's been stored in a lemonade bottle!

BATHROOM

SPOT THE POISONS!

1 After-shave	10 Toilet bowl cleaner	19 Bleach	28 Insecticide
2 Disinfectant	11 Animal medicines	20 Dishwashing liquid	29 Rat poison
3 Paint	12 Alcohol	21 Dyes	30 Brake fluid
4 Paint-stripper	13 Tobacco	22 Old cat food	31 Turpentine
5 Carpet shampoo	14 Glue	23 Laundry detergent	32 Engine oil
6 Soap	15 Air freshener	24 Shoe polish	33 Kerosene
7 Bubble bath liquid	16 Lighter fuel	25 Metal polish	34 Rust remover
8 Aspirin	17 Furniture polish	26 Weed killer	35 Antifreeze
9 Antiseptic	18 Ammonia	27 Fertilizer	36 Gasoline

KITCHEN

GARDEN SHED

Answer to SPOT THE POISONS: All of them could poison you!

[13]

MARY, MARY, QUITE CONTRARY

1 POISON IVY

All parts are poisonous

2 RHUBARB

Poisonous leaves

3 POTATO

Green parts are poisonous

4 DAFFODIL

Poisonous bulbs

5 LUPINE

Poisonous seeds

6 HOLLY

Poisonous leaves and berries

7 DEADLY NIGHTSHADE

Deadly poisonous

8 MONK'S HOOD

All parts are poisonous

9 BROOM

Poisonous seeds and seed pods

10 YEW

Poisonous leaves and fruit

11 FOXGLOVE

Deadly poisonous

Most gardens have poisonous plants growing in them. Here's a real horror-show garden.

12 RHODODENDRON

All of its parts are poisonous

13 WATER HEMLOCK

Deadly poisonous

14 POISON OAK

All of its parts are poisonous

15 BLACK LOCUST

Poisonous leaves and bark

16 DELPHINIUM

All of its parts are poisonous

AND THERE ARE MANY MORE!

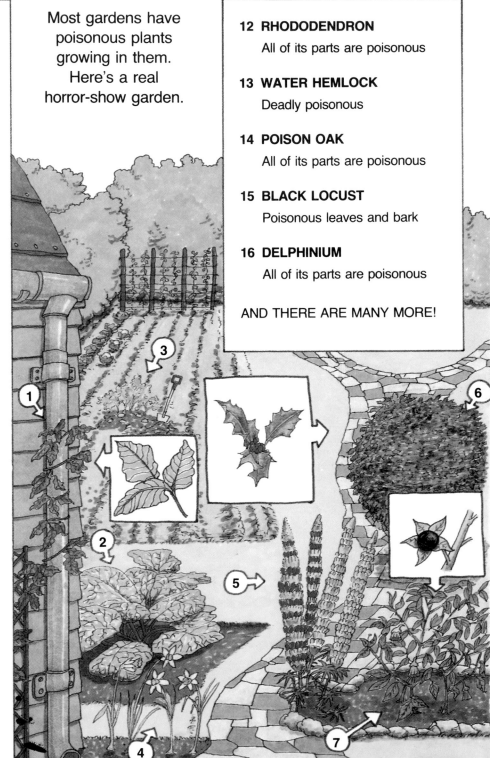

HOW DOES YOUR GARDEN GROW?

MUSHROOMS AND TOADSTOOLS

Mushrooms and toadstools are kinds of fungi.
There are thousands of different sorts of fungi.
Some are too small to be seen. There could be one here!

Some fungi contain deadly poisons!
WHAT HAPPENS IF YOU EAT THESE?

DESTROYING ANGEL
Looks a lot like a mushroom from
a market, but it's deadly poisonous!

DEATH CAP
No known cure for this one!
It causes many deaths.

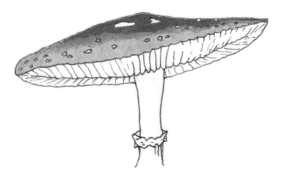

FLY AGARIC
Not always deadly, but it makes
you go mad!

COMMON INK CAP
Good to eat except if you drink alcohol
as well. Then it makes you sick!

Poisonous mushrooms often look like ones you can eat.
So it's best if you eat only mushrooms you buy from a shop.

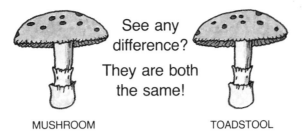

See any
difference?
They are both
the same!

MUSHROOM

TOADSTOOL

The word toadstool is often used to describe
a mushroom that's poisonous.
But some mushrooms can be poisonous too!

So if you're not sure, leave wild mushrooms
and toadstools to the toads!

HELP A TOAD ACROSS THE ROAD
Here's a tired toad who needs a rest. See if you can
guide him to his stool through the traffic. He mustn't
touch any of the people or traffic or exhaust fumes!

Now that you know what a toadstool is, find out about toadfish!

CREATURES TO MAKE YOU SHUDDER AND SHAKE!

Lots of wild animals around the world are poisonous. All of these creatures are bad for your health if they get you!

CENTIPEDES AND MILLIPEDES
Usually small and harmless, but some can bite through skin and poison you!

HORNETS
They look like large wasps and give a painful sting. If they gang up on you, they can be deadly!

VENOMOUS TOADFISH
Lives in the Atlantic Ocean and can grow up to about 20 inches (50 centimeters) long. It has poisonous spines!

STING RAY
Lives near the coasts of Europe, America, and Africa. Has poisonous spines!

WEEVER FISH
It often buries itself in the sand on the sea floor. It has poisonous spines, so it's very painful if you step on it!

CREATURES TO MAKE YOU SHUDDER AND SHAKE!

SCORPION
If you're in a hot country, make sure one hasn't crept into your shoe during the night. A scorpion sting can be deadly!

TREE FROG
Some South American tree frogs have a deadly poison on their skin to protect themselves from other animals!

Rivet Croak Rivet!

BLUE-RINGED OCTOPUS
Lives in warm seas near Australia. Its bite is deadly!

PORTUGUESE MAN-OF-WAR
Floats on the sea. Has poisonous tentacles up to 100 feet (30 meters) long!

SEA URCHINS
They live on rocks under water. If you step on one, the spines break off in your skin and poison you!

And there's more!

ARE YOU SCARED OF **SPIDERS!?**

Don't be! Most spiders are harmless to humans.

But there are a few that have poisonous bites that are deadly! If you think you've been bitten by one of those, it's best if a doctor sees you.

TARANTULA
Found in tropical parts of the world. They have been known to hide in bunches of bananas, so they can turn up in cooler parts of the world too!

FUNNEL WEB SPIDER
An Australian spider that has a killer bite. They like to live in cobwebby tunnels under stones and logs.

BLACK WIDOW SPIDER
Found in warm areas all over the world. Its bite can be deadly.

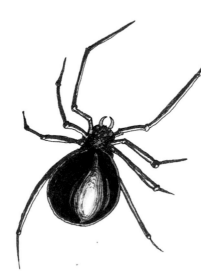

When spiders bite, they usually inject a poison that stops the victim from moving, so the victim can't escape.

Some spiders store captured insects in a sort of larder made of cobwebs.

SNAKES!?

Some snakes have hollow teeth so that they can inject their victims with poison. Snake poison is called venom.

Two sharp hollow teeth called fangs inject venom like a syringe

Some snakes have a special organ which helps them to detect the heat given off by their prey

Venom sac under the fangs

A forked tongue tastes the air to find food

A RATTLESNAKE

SNAKE FACT	SNAKE FACT	SNAKE FACT
Snakes don't sting, they bite!	Some snake venom can stop your heart!	Many snakebites are harmless!

If you're bitten by a snake, don't panic!

Don't rush about! Running makes the blood flow around your body more quickly. That means the venom will soon reach your heart. Try not to move the part that's been bitten. Somebody will have to bring a doctor to see you. There are cures for most snakebites.

ZZZZ!

YOW!
A snake!

Some people die of fright when they are bitten by harmless snakes or wasps!

SO GET TO KNOW YOUR SNAKES!

SNAKES AND ADDERS

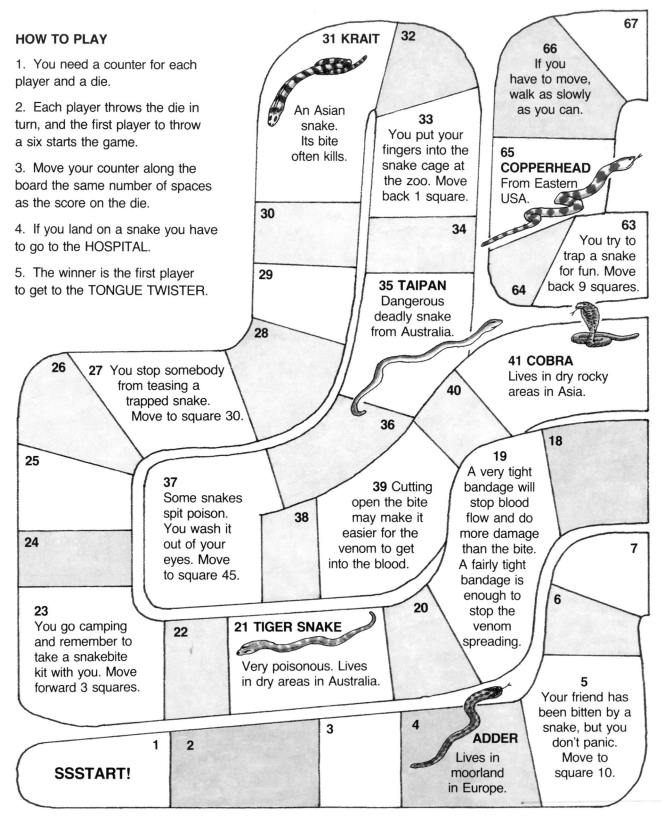

HOW TO PLAY

1. You need a counter for each player and a die.

2. Each player throws the die in turn, and the first player to throw a six starts the game.

3. Move your counter along the board the same number of spaces as the score on the die.

4. If you land on a snake you have to go to the HOSPITAL.

5. The winner is the first player to get to the TONGUE TWISTER.

31 KRAIT
An Asian snake. Its bite often kills.

32

33
You put your fingers into the snake cage at the zoo. Move back 1 square.

34

35 TAIPAN
Dangerous deadly snake from Australia.

67

66
If you have to move, walk as slowly as you can.

65 COPPERHEAD
From Eastern USA.

63
You try to trap a snake for fun. Move back 9 squares.

64

41 COBRA
Lives in dry rocky areas in Asia.

40

36

30

29

28

26

27 You stop somebody from teasing a trapped snake. Move to square 30.

25

24

37
Some snakes spit poison. You wash it out of your eyes. Move to square 45.

38

39 Cutting open the bite may make it easier for the venom to get into the blood.

19
A very tight bandage will stop blood flow and do more damage than the bite. A fairly tight bandage is enough to stop the venom spreading.

18

7

6

20

23
You go camping and remember to take a snakebite kit with you. Move forward 3 squares.

22

21 TIGER SNAKE
Very poisonous. Lives in dry areas in Australia.

5
Your friend has been bitten by a snake, but you don't panic. Move to square 10.

1 **2**

3

4

ADDER
Lives in moorland in Europe.

SSSTART!

[22]

SNAKES AND ADDERS

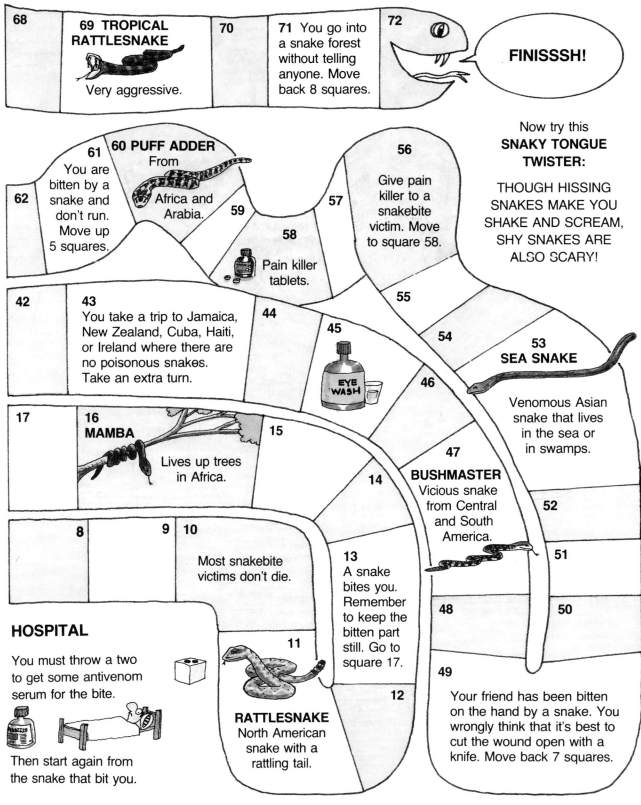

68

69 TROPICAL RATTLESNAKE
Very aggressive.

70

71 You go into a snake forest without telling anyone. Move back 8 squares.

72

FINISSSH!

Now try this
SNAKY TONGUE TWISTER:

THOUGH HISSING SNAKES MAKE YOU SHAKE AND SCREAM, SHY SNAKES ARE ALSO SCARY!

61 You are bitten by a snake and don't run. Move up 5 squares.

60 PUFF ADDER From Africa and Arabia.

62

59

58 Pain killer tablets.

56 Give pain killer to a snakebite victim. Move to square 58.

57

55

54

53 SEA SNAKE
Venomous Asian snake that lives in the sea or in swamps.

42

43 You take a trip to Jamaica, New Zealand, Cuba, Haiti, or Ireland where there are no poisonous snakes. Take an extra turn.

44

45
EYE WASH

46

47 BUSHMASTER
Vicious snake from Central and South America.

52

17

16 MAMBA
Lives up trees in Africa.

15

14

51

8

9

10 Most snakebite victims don't die.

13 A snake bites you. Remember to keep the bitten part still. Go to square 17.

48

50

HOSPITAL

You must throw a two to get some antivenom serum for the bite.

Then start again from the snake that bit you.

11

RATTLESNAKE
North American snake with a rattling tail.

12

49 Your friend has been bitten on the hand by a snake. You wrongly think that it's best to cut the wound open with a knife. Move back 7 squares.

TOBACCO

Some crazy people poison themselves on purpose!

People who smoke are poisoning themselves with all sorts of terrible toxic chemicals.

So smokers may get any of these serious illnesses.

Loss of senses of taste and smell

Bad breath

Heart disease

Ulcers and stomach cancer

Weak muscles

Blood clots

Throat cancer

Bronchitis

Lung cancer

Bad blood circulation

Empty wallet!

SPOT THE SMOKER. Can you guess which of these people smokes?

Being in the same room as a smoker can be harmful to you too!

ANSWER TO SPOT THE SMOKER: THE ONE IN THE AMBULANCE OF COURSE!

TOBACCO FACTS!

Tobacco smoke makes clothes smell horrible!

It's against the law to sell tobacco to minors in most of the United States.

Many house fires are started by smokers leaving cigarette ends burning!

Tobacco smoke contains over 4,000 different chemicals. Many of these are poisonous! For example . . .

NICOTINE is one of the deadliest poisons in the world. It affects the heart and the nerves!

About 360,000 people die in the United States each year of causes related to smoking.

TAR is an evil-smelling brown substance that blocks the lungs!

CARBON MONOXIDE replaces the oxygen in the blood, so that smokers easily get out of breath!

Work out how much a 20-a-day smoker spends on tobacco in 30 years.

Some people even poison themselves twice, by smoking and by drinking alcohol!

ALCOHOL

Alcohol is a poison that people drink. It's in . . .

BEER

WINE

LIQUOR

People who drink a lot often smoke a lot, too!

Alcohol can make you feel happy for a while, but it often makes you feel sick later on.

And alcohol can even make you feel tired, too!

Small amounts of alcohol aren't dangerous. Some health experts say that a glass of wine each day is good for you. But drinking too much is bad for you.

SPOT THE DRUNK
One of these people drinks too much alcohol.
See if you can tell which one it is.

 Alcohol changes people's behavior. Quiet, harmless people can become violent if they drink too much!

 Drinking too much makes people drive dangerously. That's why drinking and driving is against the law.

ANSWER TO SPOT THE DRUNK: THE ONE BEING SICK IS THE DRUNK!

BOOZY BUSINESS

It's against the law to sell alcohol to people under 21 years old!

Alcohol is produced by the fungus called yeast. Just as some mushrooms make deadly poisons, yeast makes alcohol, which can poison people who drink a lot!

Alcohol can damage the blood vessels in your skin, so that some people who drink too much get big red noses!

Mine's bigger than yours!

Your liver helps to remove poisons from your body by cleaning the blood. Alcohol can damage the liver so that it doesn't work properly. That means that the blood becomes clogged up with other poisons, too!

Some people lose their memory after drinking alcohol!

Alcohol can destroy brain cells!

In the United States about 100,000 people die each year from injuries and illnesses related to alcohol.

eek!

Alcohol can damage blood vessels in your leg. Then your toes might drop off!

Alcohol is addictive. That means that some people can't do without it. They have to get medical help to stop drinking.

Other things are addictive, too!

[27]

DRUGS

Drugs are substances that affect the body. They are often used by doctors as painkillers or to help cure a patient. Most drugs are poisonous if used wrongly, even those that doctors give to their patients. But some drugs are too dangerous to use at all. So it's against the law to use them. Here are four dangerous drugs that are banned by law.

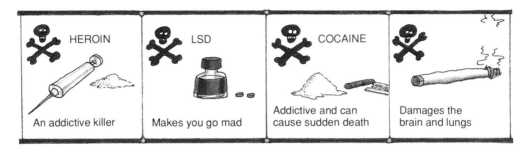

HEROIN
An addictive killer

LSD
Makes you go mad

COCAINE
Addictive and can cause sudden death

Damages the brain and lungs

SPOT THE DRUG-TAKERS
Which two of these people use drugs that are against the law?

Banned drugs can also contain all sorts of other poisons! This is because they are produced and sold by people who don't care about other people's lives. The police once found a stash of marijuana that was mixed with horse manure!

ANSWER TO SPOT THE DRUG-TAKERS:
THE ONE WHO THINKS SHE CAN FLY AND THE ONE STEALING TO GET MONEY TO BUY DRUGS!

DEADLY DRUG DATA

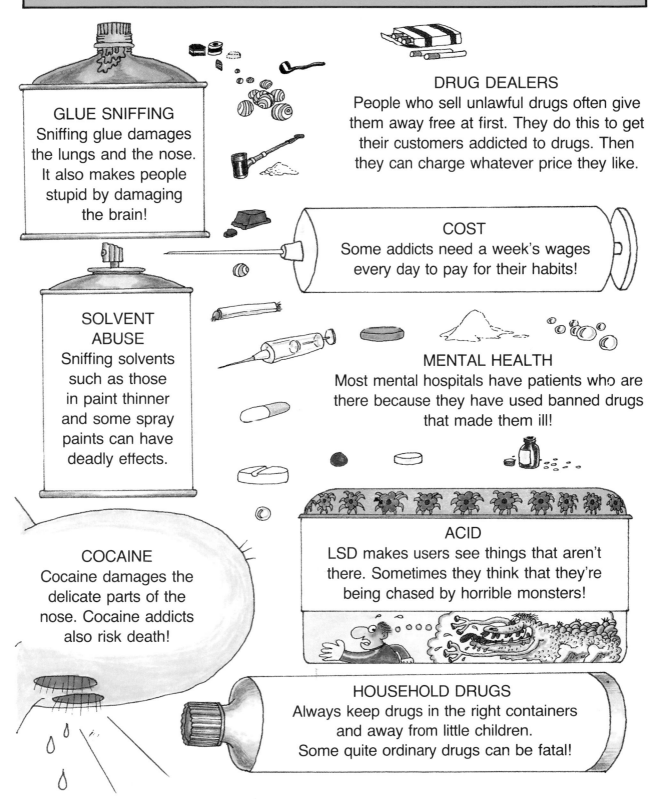

GLUE SNIFFING
Sniffing glue damages the lungs and the nose. It also makes people stupid by damaging the brain!

DRUG DEALERS
People who sell unlawful drugs often give them away free at first. They do this to get their customers addicted to drugs. Then they can charge whatever price they like.

COST
Some addicts need a week's wages every day to pay for their habits!

SOLVENT ABUSE
Sniffing solvents such as those in paint thinner and some spray paints can have deadly effects.

MENTAL HEALTH
Most mental hospitals have patients who are there because they have used banned drugs that made them ill!

COCAINE
Cocaine damages the delicate parts of the nose. Cocaine addicts also risk death!

ACID
LSD makes users see things that aren't there. Sometimes they think that they're being chased by horrible monsters!

HOUSEHOLD DRUGS
Always keep drugs in the right containers and away from little children. Some quite ordinary drugs can be fatal!

SNACKS AND ADDITIVES

AARGH!

When was the last time you ate some BUTYLATED HYDROXYANISOLE?

You've probably eaten some in the last few days! This is one of many chemicals that are put in all sorts of foods.

WOW!

FRUIT DRINKS

PICKLES

BREADS

COOKIES

POTATO CHIPS

PIE FILLINGS

SOUP MIXES

SALAD DRESSINGS

ADDITIVES

ADDITIVES LAB (PIES DEPT)

Chemicals that food scientists add to food are called additives.

Additives are put into food for lots of reasons:

To make food look attractive
To make food last longer
To make mushy food more solid
To make poor quality food taste better

ERGH!

Who's that?

Additives help food makers to sell their products. But additives can also make people ill. For example, some people think additives in candy can make young people violent or nervous!

It's crazy Carl. He's been eating additives again.

SNACKS AND ADDITIVES

Some additives
can give you

SKIN RASHES

STOMACH
UPSETS

TROUBLE
WITH BREATHING

NYEEG!

URRRP!

COUGH!

In the United States, laws require food makers to prove that additives are safe before they are used in food. The federal Food and Drug Administration enforces these laws.

Laws also require food labels and packages to list the ingredients of the food inside. If you want to know what's in your food, read the label!

Here's what you might find in a candy bar:

Contains sugar, corn syrup, hydrogenated palm kernel and/or coconut and/or soybean and/or peanut oil, milk, high fructose corn syrup, cocoa, dextrose, buttermilk solids, salt, skim milk, sorbitol, emulsifiers (soy lecithin and glyceryl-lacto esters of fatty acids), artificial and natural flavor, glycerin, citric acid, caramel color.

Have a look around your house for lists of additives on packages. There are hundreds of different additives. Most of them are not bad for you. But many people like to avoid additives when they can!

HOW TO EAT GERMS

Germs are very small creatures. Some are plants, and some are tiny animals. Plantlike germs are called bacteria. There are billions of bacteria in the world. Most of them are harmless. Some of them are good for us! Some bacteria are amazingly small!

BACTERIA FACT
Some bacteria live in our stomachs. They help us to digest our food!

One million bacteria on a pinhead!

Some bacteria that live in food can give you

ooh!

BELLYACHE

urrrp!

SICKNESS

BACTERIA BRAIN BOGGLER FACT
Bacteria can be attacked by even smaller forms of life called viruses!

DIARRHEA

HEADACHE

I think I've got a cold coming on!

Cold virus

SWEATING

And some bacteria that live in food produce DEADLY POISON!

HOW TO EAT GERMS

Bacteria are so small that you need a microscope to see them. A microscope works like a powerful magnifying glass.

Here are some ways food can be invaded by bacteria.

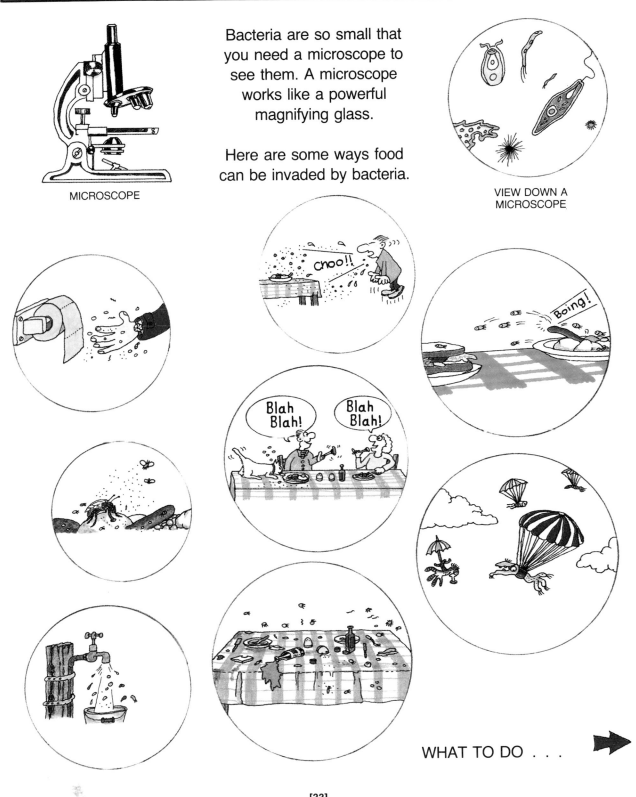

MICROSCOPE

VIEW DOWN A MICROSCOPE

WHAT TO DO . . .

HOW TO BEAT GERMS!

Bacteria like warm places but can't stand too much heat. So cooking makes some foods safer to eat.

Bacteria are killed between 145° and 212° Fahrenheit (63° and 100° Celsius).

Bacteria grow very quickly at the temperature of the human body—98.6° Fahrenheit (37° Celsius).

At 32° Fahrenheit (0° Celsius), bacteria are asleep.

You have to be especially careful with all these foods . . .

. . . because some of the most deadly bacteria can live in these products.

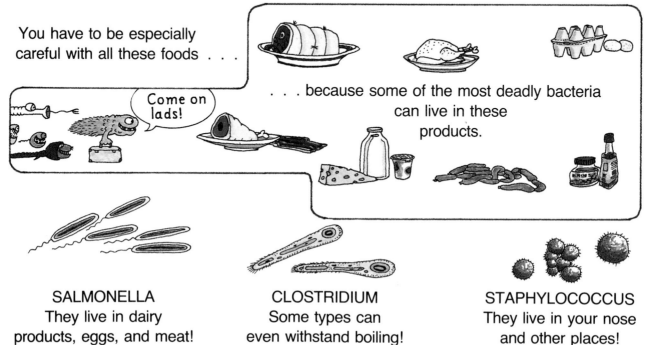

SALMONELLA
They live in dairy products, eggs, and meat!

CLOSTRIDIUM
Some types can even withstand boiling!

STAPHYLOCOCCUS
They live in your nose and other places!

Here are a few basic rules that will help you to cut down the risk of food poisoning:

Wash your hands before touching food!

Don't just warm up leftovers! Leftovers must be cooked properly!

Keep all your kitchen tools and surfaces clean! Use hot soapy water!

Make sure that frozen food is thawed out before you cook it!

Make sure that food is properly cooked before you eat it!

Don't store cooked and raw meat together!

LOOK! If you spot anyone breaking these rules, leap into action and save yourself and others from deadly poisons.

HOW TO BE A LIFESAVER

It's not easy to tell if somebody's been poisoned. But there are some clues.

WHAT TO LOOK FOR

A poison such as mushrooms, aspirin, or weed killer is nearby, or the person's mouth might be stained, or the person is asleep and can't be woken up.

WHAT TO DO

If the person is asleep and can't be woken up . . .

Don't panic! Call a doctor or emergency service right away!
Take out anything that's loose in the person's mouth, so that the person won't choke. That includes false teeth!
Save any poison you find nearby to show the doctor!
Don't try to make the person vomit!
Try to get the person into the recovery position if you are strong enough!
Keep the person warm and comfortable!

SEE PAGE 37 FOR THE RECOVERY POSITION

If the person is awake . . .

Don't panic! Call a doctor or emergency service right away!
Give the poisoned person lots of water or milk to drink!
Keep the person awake, comfortable, and warm!
Save any poison you find nearby to show the doctor!

HOW TO BE A LIFESAVER

Lying in the recovery position is the best way for an unconscious person to breathe. Unconscious people are almost impossible to move. Don't try too long before you call a doctor.

THE
RECOVERY
POSITION

There's a lot more to know about first aid. Go and see your local Red Cross branch or first aid group to find out!

Here are two more poisons you can save people from.

SMOKE from house fires is deadly! When soft furniture catches fire, the smoke given off is a killer. If you can smell it, you're already being poisoned!

WHAT TO DO

GET OUT
AND CALL THE
FIRE DEPARTMENT

If you crawl, you may be able to get out under the smoke. A damp cloth will stop some of the smoke or gas from reaching your lungs.

GAS leaks are deadly! If you smell gas DON'T LIGHT A MATCH OR SWITCH ON A LIGHT! It might cause an explosion!

WHAT TO DO

GET OUT
AND CALL THE
GAS COMPANY

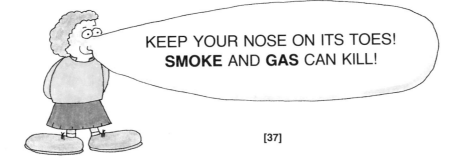

KEEP YOUR NOSE ON ITS TOES!
SMOKE AND **GAS** CAN KILL!

THE ACE POISON SPOTTER SAYS

**DON'T PUT THINGS
YOU AREN'T SURE ABOUT
IN YOUR MOUTH!**

You'll probably see some of the poisons in this book
every day. Some are a lot less common.

But now that you're an expert on poisons, you'll be
safe from most of them!
And you'll know when to leap into action to save
other people's insides!

ONE MORE THING:

**DON'T EAT THIS BOOK!
IT MAY BE
POISONOUS!**

FIND OUT MORE

Now that you've learned how to spot poisons, find out more about how to guard against them. Here are some books to look for in the library:

Alcohol—What It Is, What It Does, by Judith S. Scixas (Greenwillow, 1981)

A Breath of Air & a Breath of Smoke, by John S. Marr (M. Evans, 1988)

Dumb Cane and Daffodils: Poisonous Plants in the House and Garden, by Carol Lerner (Morrow, 1990)

A Kid's Guide to First Aid, by Lory Freeman (Parenting Press, 1983)

Making Up Your Mind About Drugs, by Gilda Berger (Lodestar Books, 1988)

Poisonous Snakes, by Colin McCarthy (Franklin Watts, 1987)

Poisons Make You Sick, by Dorothy Chald (Childrens Press, 1984)

INDEX